Bible Study Sampler

by John & Sarita Holzmann

Bible Study
Sampler

By John & Sarita Holzmann

Published by
Sonlight Curriculum, Ltd.
8042 South Grant Way
Littleton, CO 80122-2705
(303) 730-6292 FAX (303) 795-8668
E-Mail: main@sonlight.com

For HELP: www.sonlight.com/forums/

ISBN 1-887840-54-0
ISBN 978-1-887840-54-5

Table of Contents

Introduction 7

Week 1 9

Week 2 14

Week 3 19

Week 4 24

Week 5 29

Week 6 34

Week 7 39

Week 8 44

Week 9 49

Week 10 54

Week 11 59

Week 12 64

Week 13 69

Week 14 74

Week 15 79

Week 16 84

Week 17 89

Week 18 94

Week 19 99

Week 20 104

Week 21 109

Week 22 114

Week 23 119

Week 24 124

Week 25 129

Week 26 134

Week 27 139

Week 28 144

Week 29 149

Week 30 154

Week 31 159

Week 32 164

Week 33 169

Week 34 174

Week 35 179

Week 36 184

Introduction

Welcome to Sonlight®'s Bible Study Sampler! This book will guide you through the wonders of some of the most powerful portions of the Bible and help teach you how to read the Bible in a more effective way. By following the simple instructions on these pages, you will study two passages from the Old Testament and three from the New every week. You will have the chance to dig into the meaning of various songs, sayings, biographies, prayers, and more. You'll grapple with prophecies related to Jesus, His miracles, teachings and parables. And you'll also pore over key passages from each of the New Testament letters.

What a rich book the Bible is! There is so much we can learn from reading this one book.

We hope this sampler will help you grasp some of the immeasurable treasures of the greatest Book ever written, and by understanding His words, your life will forever be changed. "Great peace have they who love your law, and nothing can make them stumble" (Psalm 119:165).

If we can assist you at any time, please do not hesitate to let us know. Take some time and visit the forums (www.sonlight.com/forums) to talk with other students and parents who are going through this same program. Or email us at main@sonlight.com, or call us at (303)730-6292 and we will be happy to help you out in any way that we can.

Report the Story

Journalists ask "Five W's and an H" when they are gathering information: Who, What, When, Where, How . . . and Why? Act as a reporter, gather the information, and report what you find.[1]

Genesis 22

Who is this story about? (Who are the main characters?) _____

_____

What happens in the story? (What is the primary conflict?) _____

_____

When does this event take place? _____

Where does it take place? (Find on a map any locations mentioned in the text.)   _____

Why do you think God included it in the Bible? _____

_____

How will you change as a result of reading this story?_____

_____

_____

---

[1] Please note: The last two questions are not the same as those that a news reporter would ask. A news reporter normally wants to know why the protagonists in their story did whatever they did; and the reporter also wants to know how the protagonists achieved their ends. We are asking rather different questions . . . about God and about you.

Wise Sayings
Proverbs 6:6-11

What analogies does this proverb use? _____

_____

What attitude or action does this text praise? _____

_____

What benefits do these proverbs promise us if we follow their advice?

_____

What attitudes or actions does this text condemn? _____

_____

What curse are we promised if we fail to heed its commands? _____

_____

The message of this proverb is . . . _____

_____

_____

_____

God Speaks Truth[2]

Please look at the Old Testament prophecies in context. Notice how the New Testament author refers to them. Is the Old Testament passage an obvious prophecy? Why or why not?

New Testament Passage	Old Testament Passage	What does the Old Testament passage predict concerning Jesus?	Obvious Prophecy? (Y/N)
Matthew 1:18-23	Isaiah 7:14		
Matthew 2:1-6[3]	Micah 5:2		
Matthew 2:7-15	Hosea 11:1		
Matthew 2:16-18	Jeremiah 31:15		
Matthew 3:1-12	Isaiah 40:3		
Matthew 4:12-17	Isaiah 9:1,2		
Matthew 8:5-17	Isaiah 53:4		
Matthew 11:2-6	Isaiah 29:18-19; 35:5-6; 61:1		
Matthew 11:7-10	Malachi 3:1		

[2] The vast majority of prophecy has to do with the prophets *forthtelling* God's standards for justice and righteousness; only a small portion of their works have to do with *foretelling* the future.

[3] Notice how Herod interprets the Magi's question about the "king of the Jews." Somehow, he, a non-Jew, knows that the "king of the Jews" is also the "Christ," the Messiah. Moreover, please note that he gets the answer he does not from Christians, but from the Jewish leaders: the "chief priests and teachers of the law."

Jesus' Words
John 3:1-21

What are Jesus' key ideas in this passage? _____

_____

_____

_____

Which verse, sentence, or phrase do you think is key to the meaning
of this passage? Why? _____

_____

_____

Which verse, sentence, or phrase bothers you or makes you stop and
think the most? What about it causes you to stop and think? _____

_____

_____

How can you apply Jesus' words in your life? How *will* you apply
what He has taught you? _____

_____

_____

Jesus' Stories
Luke 6:46-49

What title would you give this parable? _____

_____

_____

Why do you think Jesus tells this story? _____

_____

_____

What key message does Jesus teach? _____

_____

_____

How will you apply Jesus' lesson in your life? _____

_____

_____

_____

Biography

Genesis 4:1-15

Describe the primary character. List his characteristics. _____

_____

_____

What events confirm your description? _____

_____

When does this person live? _____

Where does he live? (Find the locations mentioned in the text.)

_____

Why do you think God included this person's biography in the Bible?

_____

_____

How do you intend to change as a result of studying this person?

_____

_____

Sing to the Lord[4]
Psalm 15

The overall message of this psalm is... _____

_____

Which line or couplet from this psalm speaks most powerfully to
you? Why? _____

_____

_____

Does any section of this psalm disturb you? Why? _____

_____

_____

Write down any promises of blessing and any promises of curses.

_____

_____

According to the psalm, what must you do to receive either the blessing or the curse? _____

Do any portions of this psalm serve as prophecy, either *forthtelling*
truths or *foretelling* future events? _____

How will you change as a result of this psalm? _____

_____

---

[4] The Psalms as poetry and songs, include everything from personal meditations to
prophecies and dialogs, praise songs to songs of complaint. With that diversity in mind,
the standard questions about psalms may work more or less powerfully.

History

Matthew 1:1-17 and

Luke 3:23-35

Compare the two lists of Jesus' ancestors. How do they differ? What clues can you find that might explain why they differ as they do? _____

_____

_____

_____

_____

What characteristics about which ancestors most startle or intrigue you? Why? _____

_____

_____

Why do you think God includes genealogies like these in the Bible?

_____

_____

_____

Jesus' Words
Matthew 5:1-16

What are Jesus' key ideas in this passage? _____

_____

_____
_____

Which verse, sentence, or phrase do you think is key to the meaning
of this passage? Why? _____

_____

_____

Which verse, sentence, or phrase bothers you or makes you stop and
think the most? What about it causes you to stop and think?_____

_____

_____

How can you apply Jesus' words in your life? How *will* you apply
what He has taught you? _____

_____

_____

Day 5   Week 2

Report the Story
Luke 2:1-20

Who is this story about? (Who are the main characters?) _____

_____

What happens in the story? (What is the primary conflict?) _____

_____

_____

When does this event take place? _____

Where does it take place? _____

Why do you think God included it in the Bible? _____

_____

_____

How do you intend to change as a result of reading this story? _____

_____

_____

Laws

Exodus 20:1-17

Rewrite each law in your own words. _____

_____

_____

_____

_____

_____

_____

_____

What promise does God give for obedience? _____

_____

What punishment does God promise for disobedience? _____

_____

What rationale does God give for each commandment? _____

_____

_____

_____

_____

What law do you need to take more seriously?_____

_____

Day 2   Week 3

Wise Sayings
Proverbs 6:16-19

What analogies does this proverb use? _____

_____

What attitude or action does this text praise? _____

_____

What benefit does this proverb promise to us if we follow its advice?

_____

What attitudes or actions does this text condemn? _____

_____

What curse are we promised if we fail to heed its commands? _____

_____

The message of this proverb is . . . _____

_____

_____

_____

Report the Story

Luke 2:22-52[5]

Retell the story of Jesus' childhood in your own words. _____

_____

_____

_____

_____

_____

_____

_____

_____

_____

_____

_____

_____

What one characteristic of Jesus impresses you the most? _____

_____

_____

[5] Details matter! In verse 24, Luke quotes from Leviticus 12:8. Look up the original; it says something significant about Joseph and Mary's economic condition. How well-off were they?

Day 4

Jesus' Words

Matthew 6:1-4; 16-34

What are Jesus' key ideas in this passage? _____

_____

_____

_____

Which verse, sentence, or phrase do you think is key to the meaning
of this passage? Why? _____

_____

_____

Which verse, sentence, or phrase bothers you or makes you stop and
think the most? What about it causes you to stop and think? _____

_____

_____

How can you apply Jesus' words in your life? How *will* you apply
what He has taught you? _____

_____

_____

Jesus' Stories

Luke 5:33-39

What title would you give this parable? _____

_____

_____

Why do you think Jesus tells this story? _____

_____

_____

What key message do you think Jesus wants to teach? _____

_____

_____

How will you apply Jesus' lesson in your life? _____

_____

_____

_____

Book Study

Jonah 1-4

Who is the main character? _____

When did this person live? _____

Where did this person live and to what places did he travel? _____

_____

_____

Summarize the main character's story. _____

_____

_____

_____

Why do you think this person's story is in the Bible? _____

_____

_____

What should you remember from this person's life as a model for
yours? _____

_____

What is the main theme of this book? _____

_____

Extra Credit: Find and read all cross references to this character. ____

_____

_____

Sing to the Lord
Psalm 1

The overall message of this psalm is... _____
_____

Which line or couplet from this psalm speaks most powerfully to
you? Why? _____
_____
_____

Does any section in this psalm disturb you? Why? _____
_____
_____

Write down any promises of blessing and any promises of curses.
_____
_____

According to the psalm, what must you do to receive either the blessings or the curses? _____

Do any portions of this psalm serve as prophecy, either *forthtelling*
truths or *foretelling* future events? _____

How will you change as a result of this psalm? _____
_____

Jesus' Words

Matthew 7

What are Jesus' key ideas in this passage? _____

_____

_____

_____

Which verse, sentence, or phrase do you think is key to the meaning
of this passage? Why? _____

_____

_____

Which verse, sentence, or phrase bothers you or makes you stop and
think the most? What about it causes you to stop and think? _____

_____

_____

How can you apply Jesus' words in your life? How *will* you apply
what He has taught you? _____

_____

_____

Songs

Luke 1:39-56
(with special emphasis on 1:46-55)

The overall message of this song is . . . _____

_____

Which line or couplet from this song speaks most powerfully to you?
Why? _____

_____

Does any section in this song disturb you? Why? _____

_____

Write down any promises of blessing and any promises of curses.

_____

_____

According to the song, what must you do to receive either the blessings or the curses? _____

_____

Do any portions of this song serve as prophecy, either *forthtelling*
truths or *foretelling* future events? _____

How will you change as a result of this song? _____

_____

Biography

Acts 4:36-37; Acts 4:12-25; Acts 9:26-27; Acts 11:19-30;
Acts 13:1-4; Acts 15:25-26; Acts 15:35-41

Describe the primary character. List his chief characteristics. _____

_____

_____

What events confirm your description? _____

_____

When does this person live?_____

Where does he live? _____

_____

Why do you think God included this person's biography in the Bible?

_____

_____

How do you intend to change as a result of studying this person? ____

_____

_____

Biography

Numbers 13-14

Describe the primary character. List his chief characteristics. _____

_____

_____

What events confirm your description? _____

_____

When does this person live? _____

Where does he live? _____

_____

Why do you think God included this person's biography in the Bible?

_____

_____

How do you intend to change as a result of studying this person? ____

_____

_____

Wise Sayings

Proverbs 16:7 & 25:21-22

What analogies do these proverbs use? _____

_____

What attitude or action do these texts praise? _____

_____

What benefits do these proverbs promise us if we follow their advice?

_____

What attitudes or actions do these texts condemn? _____

_____

What curses are we promised if we fail to heed their commands? ____

_____

The message of these proverbs is . . . _____

_____

_____

_____

Jesus' Words
John 5:1-47

What are Jesus' key ideas in this passage? _____

_____

_____

_____

Which verse, sentence, or phrase do you think is key to the meaning
of this passage? Why? _____

_____

_____

Which verse, sentence, or phrase bothers you or makes you stop and
think the most? What about it causes you to stop and think? _____

_____

_____

How can you apply Jesus' words in your life? How *will* you apply
what He has taught you? _____

_____

_____

Jesus' Stories
Luke 15:1-7

What title would you give this parable? _____

_____

_____

Why do you think Jesus tells this story? _____

_____

_____

What key message do you think Jesus wants to teach? _____

_____

_____

How will you apply Jesus' lesson in your life? _____

_____

_____

_____

Week 5 Day 5

Sermons
Acts 2:14-41

Who was the preacher? _____

List the key points of the sermon. _____

_____

_____

_____

_____

Who was the audience?_____

How did the speaker tailor the sermon to the audience?_____

_____

_____

What was the response to the sermon? _____

_____

_____

Day 1

Sing to the Lord
Psalm 139

The overall message of this psalm is..._____

_____

Which line or couplet from this psalm speaks most powerfully to
you? Why? _____

_____

_____

Does any section in this psalm disturb you? Why? _____

_____

_____

Write down any promises of blessing and any promises of curses.

_____

_____

According to the psalm, what must you do to receive either the blessings or the curses? _____

Do any portions of this psalm serve as prophecy, either *forthtelling*
truths or *foretelling* future events? _____

How will you change as a result of this psalm? _____

_____

Laws

Exodus 16:22-30

Rewrite each law in your own words. _____

_____

_____

_____

_____

_____

_____

_____

What promise does God give for obedience? _____

_____

What punishment does God promise for disobedience? _____

_____

What rationale does God give for each commandment? _____

_____

_____

_____

_____

What law do you need to take more seriously?_____

_____

Jesus' Words
John 6:22-71

What are Jesus' key ideas in this passage? _____

_____

_____

_____

Which verse, sentence, or phrase do you think is key to the meaning
of this passage? Why? _____

_____

_____

Which verse, sentence, or phrase bothers you or makes you stop and
think the most? What about it causes you to stop and think? _____

_____

_____

How can you apply Jesus' words in your life? How *will* you apply
what He has taught you? _____

_____

_____

Jesus' Actions

Read the following passages and then fill in the blanks.

Passage	What did Jesus do?	Over what does He have power and authority?
Luke 7:11-15		
John 2:1-11		
Mark 1:40-42		
Mark 4:35-41		
John 9:1-7		
Matthew 17:14-18		
Matthew 12:10-13		

Pray for Jesus to act in one of the areas in your own or someone else's life.

Letters
Romans 1:18-32

Who wrote the letter and to whom? _____

_____

Why did the author write this to the church? _____

_____

What are the key points? _____

_____

_____

What is the theme? _____

Is there a key verse? _____

How do you intend to apply this in your own life? _____

_____

_____

Book Study

Ruth

Who is the main character? _____

When did this person live? _____

Where did this person live and to what places did she travel? _____
_____
_____

Summarize the main character's story. _____
_____
_____
_____

Why do you think this person's story is in the Bible? _____
_____
_____

What should you remember from this person's life as a model for
yours? _____
_____

What is the main theme of this book? _____
_____

Extra Credit: Find and read all cross references to this character. ____
_____
_____

Wise Sayings
Proverbs 27:5,6 & 17:17

What analogies do these proverbs use? _____

_____

What attitude or action do these texts praise? _____

_____

What benefits do these proverbs promise us if we follow their advice?

_____

What attitudes or actions do these texts condemn? _____

_____

What curses are we promised if we fail to heed their commands? ____

_____

The message of these proverbs is . . . _____

_____

_____

_____

Jesus' Words
Luke 17:1-10

What are Jesus' key ideas in this passage? _____

_____

_____

_____

Which verse, sentence, or phrase do you think is key to the meaning
of this passage? Why? _____

_____

_____

Which verse, sentence, or phrase bothers you or makes you stop and
think the most? What about it causes you to stop and think? _____

_____

_____

How can you apply Jesus' words in your life? How *will* you apply
what He has taught you? _____

_____

_____

Jesus' Stories
Luke 19:11-27

What title would you give this parable? _____

_____

_____

Why do you think Jesus tells this story? _____

_____

_____

What key message do you think Jesus wants to teach? _____

_____

_____

How will you apply Jesus' lesson in your life? _____

_____

_____

_____

Letters

Romans 5:1-11

Who wrote the letter and to whom? _____

_____

Why did the author write this to the church? _____

_____

What are the key points? _____

_____

_____

What is the theme? _____

Is there a key verse? _____

How do you intend to apply this in your own life? _____

_____

_____

Day 1   Week 8

Report the Story
Joshua 6

_____

_____

_____

_____

_____

_____

_____

_____

_____

_____

_____

_____

_____

_____

_____

_____

_____

_____

_____

_____

_____

_____

_____

Sing to the Lord
Psalm 2

The overall message of this psalm is... _____

_____

Which line or couplet from this psalm speaks most powerfully to
you? Why? _____

_____

_____

Does any section in this psalm disturb you? Why? _____

_____

_____

Write down any promises of blessing and any promises of curses.

_____

_____

According to the psalm, what must you do to receive either the blessings or the curses? _____

Do any portions of this psalm serve as prophecy, either *forthtelling*
truths or *foretelling* future events? _____

How will you change as a result of this psalm? _____

Day 3   Week 8

Jesus' Words

Luke 7:1-10

What are Jesus' key ideas in this passage? _____

_____

_____

_____

Which verse, sentence, or phrase do you think is key to the meaning
of this passage? Why? _____

_____

_____

Which verse, sentence, or phrase bothers you or makes you stop and
think the most? What about it causes you to stop and think? _____

_____

_____

How can you apply Jesus' words in your life? How *will* you apply
what He has taught you? _____

_____

_____

Verse Study
John 1:14

Paraphrase the passage—Put it in your own words. _____

_____

_____

_____

Cross-reference the passage—find any other passages that help you
understand words or concepts. _____

_____

Record any insights you have gained. _____

_____

_____

_____

_____

How will you apply what you have learned? _____

_____

_____

_____

Letters

Romans 7:7-25

Who wrote the letter and to whom? _____

_____

Why did the author write this to the church? _____

_____

What are the key points? _____

_____

_____

What is the theme? _____

Is there a key verse? _____

How do you intend to apply this in your own life? _____

_____

_____

Prayer

Exodus 32:7-14

Who prays? _____

Why is the person praying? _____

_____

What happens as a result? _____

_____

_____

Write a prayer based on the pattern in the passage. _____

_____

_____

_____

_____

_____

Wise Sayings

Proverbs 4:23-27

What analogies does this proverb use? _____

_____

What attitude or action does this text praise? _____

_____

What benefits do these proverbs promise us if we follow their advice?

_____

What attitudes or actions does this text condemn? _____

_____

What curses are we promised if we fail to heed its commands? _____

_____

The message of this proverb is . . . _____

_____

_____

_____

Jesus' Words
Mark 2:15-17

What are Jesus' key ideas in this passage? _____

_____

_____

_____

Which verse, sentence, or phrase do you think is key to the meaning
of this passage? Why? _____

_____

_____

Which verse, sentence, or phrase bothers you or makes you stop and
think the most? What about it causes you to stop and think? _____

_____

_____

How can you apply Jesus' words in your life? How *will* you apply
what He has taught you? _____

_____

_____

Jesus' Stories
Mark 4:3-20

What title would you give this parable? _____

_____

_____

Why do you think Jesus tells this story? _____

_____

_____

What key message do you think Jesus wants to teach? _____

_____

_____

How will you apply Jesus' lesson in your life? _____

_____

_____

Letters

Romans 8:26-31

Who wrote the letter and to whom? _____

_____

Why did the author write this to the church? _____

_____

What are the key points? _____

_____

_____

What is the theme? _____

Is there a key verse? _____

How do you intend to apply this in your own life? _____

_____

_____

Verse Study
Joshua 1:8,9

Paraphrase the passage—Put it in your own words. _____

_____

_____

_____

Cross-reference the passage—find any other passages that help you
understand words or concepts. _____

_____

Record any insights you have gained. _____

_____

_____

_____

_____

How will you apply what you have learned? _____

_____

_____

_____

Sing to the Lord
Psalm 90

The overall message of this psalm is... _____

_____

Which line or couplet from this psalm speaks most powerfully to
you? Why? _____

_____

_____

Does any section in this psalm disturb you? Why? _____

_____

_____

Write down any promises of blessing and any promises of curses.

_____

_____

According to the psalm, what must you do to receive either the blessings or the curses? _____

Do any portions of this psalm serve as prophecy, either *forthtelling*
truths or *foretelling* future events? _____

How will you change as a result of this psalm? _____

_____

Jesus' Words
Matthew 10:24-33

What are Jesus' key ideas in this passage? _____

_____

_____

_____

Which verse, sentence, or phrase do you think is key to the meaning
of this passage? Why? _____

_____

_____

Which verse, sentence, or phrase bothers you or makes you stop and
think the most? What about it causes you to stop and think? _____

_____

_____

How can you apply Jesus' words in your life? How *will* you apply
what He has taught you? _____

_____

_____

Jesus' Words
Matthew 5:17-48

What are Jesus' key ideas in this passage? _____

_____

_____

_____

Which verse, sentence, or phrase do you think is key to the meaning
of this passage? Why? _____

_____

_____

Which verse, sentence, or phrase bothers you or makes you stop and
think the most? What about it causes you to stop and think?_____

_____

_____

How can you apply Jesus' words in your life? How *will* you apply
what He has taught you? _____

_____

_____

Letters

Romans 12:1-21

Who wrote the letter and to whom? _____

_____

Why did the author write this to the church? _____

_____

What are the key points? _____

_____

_____

What is the theme? _____

Is there a key verse? _____

How do you intend to apply this in your own life? _____

_____

_____

Report the Story
2 Samuel 12:1-23

Who is this story about? (Who are the main characters?) _____

_____

What happens in the story? (What is the primary conflict?) _____

_____

_____

When does this event take place? _____

Where does it take place? _____

Why do you think God included it in the Bible? _____

_____

_____

How do you intend to change as a result of reading this story? _____

_____

_____

Wise Sayings
Proverbs 15:1

What analogies does this proverb use? _____

_____

What attitude or action does this text praise? _____

_____

What benefits does this proverb promise us if we follow its advice?

_____

What attitudes or actions does this text condemn? _____

_____

What curses are we promised if we fail to heed its commands? _____

_____

The message of this proverb is . . . _____

_____

_____

_____

Jesus' Words

Mark 3:20-35

What are Jesus' key ideas in this passage? _____

_____

_____

_____

Which verse, sentence, or phrase do you think is key to the meaning
of this passage? Why? _____

_____

_____

Which verse, sentence, or phrase bothers you or makes you stop and
think the most? What about it causes you to stop and think? _____

_____

_____

How can you apply Jesus' words in your life? How *will* you apply
what He has taught you? _____

_____

_____

Jesus' Stories
Matthew 25:1-13

What title would you give this parable? _____

_____

_____

Why do you think Jesus tells this story? _____

_____

_____

What key message do you think Jesus wants to teach?   _____

_____

_____

How will you apply Jesus' lesson in your life?   _____

_____

_____

_____

Letters

1 Corinthians 1:18-31

Who wrote the letter and to whom? _____

_____

Why did the author write this to the church? _____

_____

What are the key points? _____

_____

_____

What is the theme? _____

Is there a key verse? _____

How do you intend to apply this in your own life? _____

_____

_____

Old Testament Kings

2 Kings 22-23

List this king's strengths and weaknesses. _____

_____

_____

How did the king's traits affect his relationship with God? _____

_____

How did the king finish his reign? _____

_____

How do your strengths and weaknesses compare to this king? _____

_____

_____

_____

Sing to the Lord
Psalm 150

The overall message of this psalm is... _____

_____

Which line or couplet from this psalm speaks most powerfully to
you? Why? _____

_____

_____

Does any section in this psalm disturb you? Why? _____

_____

_____

Write down any promises of blessing and any promises of curses.

_____

_____

According to the psalm, what must you do to receive either the blessings or the curses? _____

Do any portions of this psalm serve as prophecy, either *forthtelling*
truths or *foretelling* future events? _____

How will you change as a result of this psalm? _____

_____

Jesus' Words

Mark 7:1-23

What are Jesus' key ideas in this passage? _____

_____

_____

_____

Which verse, sentence, or phrase do you think is key to the meaning
of this passage? Why? _____

_____

_____

Which verse, sentence, or phrase bothers you or makes you stop and
think the most? What about it causes you to stop and think? _____

_____

_____

How can you apply Jesus' words in your life? How *will* you apply
what He has taught you? _____

_____

_____

Prayer

Matthew 6:5-15

What attitudes should we have when we pray? _____

_____

_____

_____

What does Jesus teach us each prayer should include? _____

_____

_____

_____

_____

_____

Write a prayer based on the pattern Jesus gives. _____

_____

_____

_____

_____

Letters

1 Corinthians 12:1-11

Who wrote the letter and to whom? _____

_____

Why did the author write this to the church? _____

_____

What are the key points? _____

_____

_____

What is the theme? _____

Is there a key verse? _____

How do you intend to apply this in your own life? _____

_____

_____

Report the Story
Exodus 3

_____

_____

_____

_____

_____

_____

_____

_____

_____

_____

_____

_____

_____

_____

_____

_____

_____

_____

_____

_____

Wise Sayings
Proverbs 26:18-19

What analogies does this proverb use? _____
_____

What attitude or action does this text praise? _____
_____

What benefits does this proverb promise us if we follow its advice?
_____

What attitudes or actions does this text condemn? _____
_____

What curses are we promised if we fail to heed its commands? _____
_____

The message of this proverb is . . . _____
_____
_____
_____

Jesus' Words

Matthew 16:21-28

What are Jesus' key ideas in this passage? _____

_____

_____

_____

Which verse, sentence, or phrase do you think is key to the meaning
of this passage? Why? _____

_____

_____

Which verse, sentence, or phrase bothers you or makes you stop and
think the most? What about it causes you to stop and think? _____

_____

_____

How can you apply Jesus' words in your life? How *will* you apply
what He has taught you? _____

_____

_____

Jesus' Stories
Matthew 18:21-35

What title would you give this parable? _____

_____

_____

Why do you think Jesus tells this story? _____

_____

_____

What key message do you think Jesus wants to teach? _____

_____

_____

How will you apply Jesus' lesson in your life? _____

_____

_____

_____

Letters

1 Corinthians 12:12-31

Who wrote the letter and to whom? _____

_____

Why did the author write this to the church? _____

_____

What are the key points? _____

_____

_____

What is the theme? _____

Is there a key verse? _____

How do you intend to apply this in your own life? _____

_____

_____

Verse Study

Micah 6:8

Paraphrase the passage—Put it in your own words. _____

_____

_____

_____

Cross-reference the passage—find any other passages that help you
understand words or concepts. _____

_____

Record any insights you have gained. _____

_____

_____

_____

_____

How will you apply what you have learned? _____

_____

_____

_____

Sing to the Lord
Psalm 103

The overall message of this psalm is..._____

_____

Which line or couplet from this psalm speaks most powerfully to you? Why? _____

_____

_____

Does any section in this psalm disturb you? Why? _____

_____

_____

Write down any promises of blessing and any promises of curses.

_____

_____

According to the psalm, what must you do to receive either the blessings or the curses? _____

Do any portions of this psalm serve as prophecy, either *forthtelling* truths or *foretelling* future events? _____

How will you change as a result of this psalm? _____

_____

Jesus' Words
Matthew 18:1-11

What are Jesus' key ideas in this passage? _____

_____

_____

_____

Which verse, sentence, or phrase do you think is key to the meaning
of this passage? Why? _____

_____

_____

Which verse, sentence, or phrase bothers you or makes you stop and
think the most? What about it causes you to stop and think? _____

_____

_____

How can you apply Jesus' words in your life? How *will* you apply
what He has taught you? _____

_____

_____

Biography

Luke 19:1-10

Describe the primary character. List his chief characteristics. _____

_____

_____

What events confirm your description? _____

_____

When does this person live? _____

Where does he live? _____

_____

Why do you think God included this person's biography in the Bible?

_____

_____

How do you intend to change as a result of studying this person? ____

_____

_____

Letters

1 Corinthians 15:12-58

Who wrote the letter and to whom? _____

_____

Why did the author write this to the church? _____

_____

What are the key points? _____

_____

_____

What is the theme? _____

Is there a key verse? _____

How do you intend to apply this in your own life? _____

_____

_____

Biography

2 Kings 5

Describe the primary character. List his chief characteristics. _____

_____

_____

What events confirm your description? _____

_____

When does this person live? _____

Where does he live? _____

_____

Why do you think God included this person's biography in the Bible?

_____

_____

How do you intend to change as a result of studying this person? ____

_____

_____

Wise Sayings
Proverbs 3:27-28

What analogies does this proverb use? _____

_____

What attitude or action does this text praise? _____

_____

What benefits does this proverb promise us if we follow its advice?

_____

What attitudes or actions does this text condemn? _____

_____

What curses are we promised if we fail to heed its commands? _____

_____

The message of this proverb is . . . _____

_____

_____

_____

Jesus' Words
Matthew 18:15-20

What are Jesus' key ideas in this passage? _____

_____

_____

_____

Which verse, sentence, or phrase do you think is key to the meaning
of this passage? Why? _____

_____

_____

Which verse, sentence, or phrase bothers you or makes you stop and
think the most? What about it causes you to stop and think? _____

_____

_____

How can you apply Jesus' words in your life? How *will* you apply
what He has taught you? _____

_____

_____

Jesus' Stories

Luke 10:25-37

What title would you give this parable? _____

_____

_____

Why do you think Jesus tells this story? _____

_____

_____

What key message do you think Jesus wants to teach? _____

_____

_____

How will you apply Jesus' lesson in your life? _____

_____

_____

_____

Sermons

Acts 10:34-48

Who was the preacher? _____

List the key points of the sermon. _____

_____

_____

_____

_____

Who was the audience?_____

How did the speaker tailor the sermon to the audience?_____

_____

_____

What was the response to the sermon? _____

_____

_____

Report the Story
Daniel 1

_____

_____

_____

_____

_____

_____

_____

_____

_____

_____

_____

_____

_____

_____

_____

_____

_____

_____

_____

_____

_____

_____

_____

Sing to the Lord
Psalm 100

The overall message of this psalm is... _____

_____

Which line or couplet from this psalm speaks most powerfully to you? Why? _____

_____

_____

Does any section in this psalm disturb you? Why? _____

_____

_____

Write down any promises of blessing and any promises of curses.

_____

_____

According to the psalm, what must you do to receive either the blessings or the curses? _____

Do any portions of this psalm serve as prophecy, either *forthtelling* truths or *foretelling* future events? _____

How will you change as a result of this psalm? _____

_____

Jesus' Words

Matthew 20:20-28

What are Jesus' key ideas in this passage? _____

_____

_____

_____

Which verse, sentence, or phrase do you think is key to the meaning
of this passage? Why? _____

_____

_____

Which verse, sentence, or phrase bothers you or makes you stop and
think the most? What about it causes you to stop and think? _____

_____

_____

How can you apply Jesus' words in your life? How *will* you apply
what He has taught you? _____

_____

_____

Songs

Luke 2:22-35

The overall message of this song is . . . _____

_____

Which line or couplet from this song speaks most powerfully to you?
Why? _____

_____

Does any section in this song disturb you? Why? _____

_____

Write down any promises of blessing and any promises of curses.

_____

_____

According to the song, what must you do to receive either the blessings or the curses? _____

_____

Do any portions of this song serve as prophecy, either *forthtelling*
truths or *foretelling* future events? _____

How will you change as a result of this song? _____

_____

Letters

Galatians 3

Who wrote the letter and to whom? _____

_____

Why did the author write this to the church? _____

_____

What are the key points? _____

_____

_____

What is the theme? _____

Is there a key verse? _____

How do you intend to apply this in your own life? _____

_____

_____

Prayer

1 Kings 3:5-28

Who prays? _____

Why is the person praying? _____

_____

What happens as a result? _____

_____

_____

Write a prayer based on the pattern in the passage. _____

_____

_____

_____

_____

_____

Day 2   Week 17

Wise Sayings
Proverbs 9:7-9

What analogies does this proverb use? _____

_____

What attitude or action does this text praise? _____

_____

What benefits does this proverb promise us if we follow its advice?

_____

What attitudes or actions does this text condemn? _____

_____

What curses are we promised if we fail to heed its commands? _____

_____

The message of this proverb is . . . _____

_____

_____

_____

Jesus' Words
Matthew 22:15-46

What are Jesus' key ideas in this passage? _____

_____

_____

_____

Which verse, sentence, or phrase do you think is key to the meaning
of this passage? Why? _____

_____

_____

Which verse, sentence, or phrase bothers you or makes you stop and
think the most? What about it causes you to stop and think? _____

_____

_____

How can you apply Jesus' words in your life? How *will* you apply
what He has taught you? _____

_____

_____

Jesus' Stories
Matthew 13:44-50

What title would you give these parables? _____

_____

_____

Why do you think Jesus tells these stories? _____

_____

_____

What key message do you think Jesus wants to teach? _____

_____

_____

How will you apply Jesus' lesson in your life? _____

_____

_____

_____

Letters

Ephesians 4:1-16

Who wrote the letter and to whom? _____

_____

Why did the author write this to the church? _____

_____

What are the key points? _____

_____

_____

What is the theme? _____

Is there a key verse? _____

How do you intend to apply this in your own life? _____

_____

_____

Wise Sayings
Proverbs 31:10-31

Write the key points. _____

_____

_____

_____

_____

Highlight the key verse. _____

Who is the passage written to?_____

How will you apply the passage?_____

_____

_____

_____

Sing to the Lord
Psalm 19

The overall message of this psalm is... _____

_____

Which line or couplet from this psalm speaks most powerfully to
you? Why? _____

_____

_____

Does any section in this psalm disturb you? Why? _____

_____

_____

Write down any promises of blessing and any promises of curses.

_____

_____

According to the psalm, what must you do to receive either the blessings or the curses? _____

Do any portions of this psalm serve as prophecy, either *forthtelling*
truths or *foretelling* future events? _____

How will you change as a result of this psalm? _____

_____

Jesus' Words
Luke 7:36-50

What are Jesus' key ideas in this passage? _____

_____

_____

_____

Which verse, sentence, or phrase do you think is key to the meaning
of this passage? Why? _____

_____

_____

Which verse, sentence, or phrase bothers you or makes you stop and
think the most? What about it causes you to stop and think? _____

_____

_____

How can you apply Jesus' words in your life? How *will* you apply
what He has taught you? _____

_____

_____

Verse Study
Matthew 9:37-38

Paraphrase the passage—put it in your own words. _____

_____

_____

_____

Cross-reference the passage—find any other passages that help you understand words or concepts. _____

_____

Record any insights you have gained. _____

_____

_____

_____

_____

How will you apply what you have learned? _____

_____

_____

_____

Letters
Ephesians 6:10-20

Who wrote the letter and to whom? _____

_____

Why did the author write this to the church? _____

_____

What are the key points? _____

_____

_____

What is the theme? _____

Is there a key verse? _____

How do you intend to apply this in your own life? _____

_____

_____

Book Study
Obadiah

Who is the main character? _____

When did this person live? _____

Where did this person live and to what places did he travel? _____
_____
_____

Summarize the main character's story. _____
_____
_____
_____

Why do you think this person's story is in the Bible? _____
_____
_____

What should you remember from this person's life as a model for
yours? _____
_____

What is the main theme of this book? _____
_____

Extra Credit: Find and read all cross references to this character.
_____

Wise Sayings

Proverbs 3:9,10

What analogies does this proverb use? _____

_____

What attitude or action does this text praise? _____

_____

What benefits does this proverb promise us if we follow its advice?

_____

What attitudes or actions does this text condemn? _____

_____

What curses are we promised if we fail to heed its commands? _____

_____

The message of this proverb is . . . _____

_____

_____

_____

Jesus' Words

Mark 12:41-44

What are Jesus' key ideas in this passage? _____

_____

_____

_____

Which verse, sentence, or phrase do you think is key to the meaning
of this passage? Why? _____

_____

_____

Which verse, sentence, or phrase bothers you or makes you stop and
think the most? What about it causes you to stop and think? _____

_____

_____

How can you apply Jesus' words in your life? How *will* you apply
what He has taught you? _____

_____

_____

Jesus' Stories
Luke 15:11-32

What title would you give these parables? _____

_____

_____

Why do you think Jesus tells these stories? _____

_____

_____

What key message do you think Jesus wants to teach? _____

_____

_____

How will you apply Jesus' lesson in your life? _____

_____

_____

Letters

Philippians 2:1-18

Who wrote the letter and to whom? _____

_____

Why did the author write this to the church? _____

_____

What are the key points? _____

_____

_____

What is the theme? _____

Is there a key verse? _____

How do you intend to apply this in your own life? _____

_____

_____

Verse Study

1 Samuel 16:7

Paraphrase the passage—put it in your own words. _____

_____

_____

_____

Cross-reference the passage—find any other passages that help you
understand words or concepts. _____

_____

Record any insights you have gained. _____

_____

_____

_____

_____

How will you apply what you have learned? _____

_____

_____

_____

Sing to the Lord
Psalm 8

The overall message of this psalm is..._____

_____

Which line or couplet from this psalm speaks most powerfully to
you? Why? _____

_____

_____

Does any section in this psalm disturb you? Why? _____

_____

_____

Write down any promises of blessing and any promises of curses.

_____

_____

According to the psalm, what must you do to receive either the blessings or the curses? _____

Do any portions of this psalm serve as prophecy, either *forthtelling*
truths or *foretelling* future events? _____

How will you change as a result of this psalm? _____

_____

Jesus' Words

Luke 9:57-62

What are Jesus' key ideas in this passage? _____

_____

_____

_____

Which verse, sentence, or phrase do you think is key to the meaning
of this passage? Why? _____

_____

_____

Which verse, sentence, or phrase bothers you or makes you stop and
think the most? What about it causes you to stop and think? _____

_____

_____

How can you apply Jesus' words in your life? How *will* you apply
what He has taught you? _____

_____

_____

Jesus' Actions

Passage	What did Jesus do?	Over what does He have power and authority?
Luke 5:4-11		
Luke 8:43-48		
Mark 5:1-15		
Mark 5 22-24; 38-43		
John 5: 1-9		
John 6:5-13		

Read the following passages and then fill in the blanks.

Pray for Jesus to act in one of the areas in your own or someone else's life.

Letters

Colossians 3:1-17

Who wrote the letter and to whom? _____

_____

Why did the author write this to the church? _____

_____

What are the key points? _____

_____

_____

What is the theme? _____

Is there a key verse? _____

How do you intend to apply this in your own life? _____

_____

_____

Report the Story

Judges 4

Wise Sayings
Proverbs 12:15 & 19:20

What analogies do these proverbs use? _____

_____

What attitude or action does these texts praise? _____

_____

What benefits do these proverbs promise us if we follow their advice?

_____

What attitudes or actions do these texts condemn? _____

_____

What curses are we promised if we fail to heed their commands? ____

_____

The message of these proverbs is . . . _____

_____

_____

_____

Jesus' Words

Luke 11:5-13

What are Jesus' key ideas in this passage? _____

_____

_____

_____

Which verse, sentence, or phrase do you think is key to the meaning
of this passage? Why? _____

_____

_____

Which verse, sentence, or phrase bothers you or makes you stop and
think the most? What about it causes you to stop and think? _____

_____

_____

How can you apply Jesus' words in your life? How *will* you apply
what He has taught you? _____

_____

_____

Jesus' Stories
Matthew 22:1-14

What title would you give this parable? _____

_____

_____

Why do you think Jesus tells this story? _____

_____

_____

What key message do you think Jesus wants to teach? _____

_____

_____

How will you apply Jesus' lesson in your life? _____

_____

_____

_____

Verse Study
Philippians 4:6,7

Paraphrase the passage—put it in your own words. _____

_____

_____

_____

Cross-reference the passage—find any other passages that help you
understand words or concepts. _____

_____

Record any insights you have gained. _____

_____

_____

_____

_____

How will you apply what you have learned? _____

_____

_____

_____

Biography

Judges 13-16

Describe the primary character. List his chief characteristics. _____

_____

_____

What events confirm your description? _____

_____

When does this person live? _____

Where does he live? _____

_____

Why do you think God included this person's biography in the Bible?

_____

_____

How do you intend to change as a result of studying this person? ____

_____

_____

Sing to the Lord
Psalm 27

The overall message of this psalm is... _____

_____

Which line or couplet from this psalm speaks most powerfully to you? Why? _____

_____

_____

Does any section in this psalm disturb you? Why? _____

_____

_____

Write down any promises of blessing and any promises of curses.

_____

_____

According to the psalm, what must you do to receive either the blessings or the curses? _____

Do any portions of this psalm serve as prophecy, either *forthtelling* truths or *foretelling* future events? _____

How will you change as a result of this psalm? _____

_____

Jesus' Words
Luke 12:49-59

What are Jesus' key ideas in this passage? _____

_____

_____

_____

Which verse, sentence, or phrase do you think is key to the meaning
of this passage? Why? _____

_____

_____

Which verse, sentence, or phrase bothers you or makes you stop and
think the most? What about it causes you to stop and think? _____

_____

_____

How can you apply Jesus' words in your life? How *will* you apply
what He has taught you? _____

_____

_____

Report the Story

Matthew 4:1-11

Who is this story about? (Who are the main characters?) _____

_____

What happens in the story? (What is the primary conflict?) _____

_____

_____

When does this event take place? _____

Where does it take place?_____

Why do you think God included it in the Bible? _____

_____

_____

How do you intend to change as a result of reading this story? _____

_____

_____

Letters

1 Thessalonians 5:12-28

Who wrote the letter and to whom? _____

_____

Why did the author write this to the church? _____

_____

What are the key points? _____

_____

_____

What is the theme? _____

Is there a key verse? _____

How do you intend to apply this in your own life? _____

_____

_____ . _____

Laws

Malachi 3:8-12

Rewrite each law in your own words. _____

_____

_____

_____

_____

_____

_____

_____

What promise does God give for obedience? _____

_____

What punishment does God promise for disobedience? _____

_____

What rationale does God give for each commandment? _____

_____

_____

_____

_____

What law do you need to take more seriously?_____

_____

Wise Sayings
Proverbs 17:22 & 14:30

What analogies do these proverbs use? _____

_____

What attitude or action do these texts praise? _____

_____

What benefits do these proverbs promise us if we follow their advice?

_____

What attitudes or actions do these texts condemn? _____

_____

What curses are we promised if we fail to heed their commands? ____

_____

The message of these proverbs is . . . _____

_____

_____

_____

Week 23 Day 3

Jesus' Words
Luke 14:25-35

What are Jesus' key ideas in this passage? _____

_____

_____

_____

Which verse, sentence, or phrase do you think is key to the meaning
of this passage? Why? _____

_____

_____

Which verse, sentence, or phrase bothers you or makes you stop and
think the most? What about it causes you to stop and think? _____

_____

_____

How can you apply Jesus' words in your life? How *will* you apply
what He has taught you? _____

_____

_____

Jesus' Stories

Luke 16:1-13

What title would you give this parable? _____

_____

_____

Why do you think Jesus tells this story? _____

_____

_____

What key message do you think Jesus wants to teach? _____

_____

_____

How will you apply Jesus' lesson in your life? _____

_____

_____

_____

Letters

2 Thessalonians 3

Who wrote the letter and to whom? _____

_____

Why did the author write this to the church? _____

_____

What are the key points? _____

_____

_____

What is the theme? _____

Is there a key verse? _____

How do you intend to apply this in your own life? _____

_____

_____

Book Study

Haggai

When did this story occur? _____

Where did the main characters live? _____

What is the main theme of this book? _____
_____

Who are the main characters? _____
_____

What is the main character's story? _____
_____

Read the cross-references to Zerubbabel son of Shealtiel and to the prophet Haggai. (See Ezra 3: 1-9; 5: 1, 2; 6: 14.)

Why is this book in the Bible? _____
_____

What will you apply to your life? _____
_____
_____

Sing to the Lord
Psalm 32

The overall message of this psalm is... _____

_____

Which line or couplet from this psalm speaks most powerfully to
you? Why? _____

_____

_____

Does any section in this psalm disturb you? Why? _____

_____

_____

Write down any promises of blessing and any promises of curses.

_____

_____

According to the psalm, what must you do to receive either the blessings or the curses? _____

Do any portions of this psalm serve as prophecy, either *forthtelling*
truths or *foretelling* future events? _____

How will you change as a result of this psalm? _____

_____

Jesus' Words
John 4:1-42

What are Jesus' key ideas in this passage? _____

_____

_____

_____

Which verse, sentence, or phrase do you think is key to the meaning of this passage? Why? _____

_____

_____

Which verse, sentence, or phrase bothers you or makes you stop and think the most? What about it causes you to stop and think? _____

_____

_____

How can you apply Jesus' words in your life? How *will* you apply what He has taught you? _____

_____

_____

Jesus' Words
Matthew 19:16-30

What are Jesus' key ideas in this passage? _____

_____

_____

_____

Which verse, sentence, or phrase do you think is key to the meaning
of this passage? Why? _____

_____

_____

Which verse, sentence, or phrase bothers you or makes you stop and
think the most? What about it causes you to stop and think? _____

_____

_____

How can you apply Jesus' words in your life? How *will* you apply
what He has taught you? _____

_____

Letters

1 Timothy 2

Who wrote the letter and to whom? _____

_____

Why did the author write this to the church? _____

_____

What are the key points? _____

_____

_____

What is the theme? _____

Is there a key verse? _____

How do you intend to apply this in your own life? _____

_____

_____

Report the Story

1 Samuel 20

Who is this story about? (Who are the main characters?) _____

_____

What happens in the story? (What is the primary conflict?) _____

_____

_____

When does this event take place? _____

Where does it take place?_____

Why do you think God included it in the Bible? _____

_____

_____

How do you intend to change as a result of reading this story? _____

_____

_____

Wise Sayings
Proverbs 16:18

What analogies do these proverbs use? _____

_____

What attitude or action do these texts praise? _____

_____

What benefits does this proverb promise us if we follow its advice?

_____

What attitudes or actions do these texts condemn? _____

_____

What curses are we promised if we fail to heed their commands? ____

_____

The message of these proverbs is . . . _____

_____

_____

_____

Jesus' Words
John 7:14-44

What are Jesus' key ideas in this passage? _____

_____

_____

_____

Which verse, sentence, or phrase do you think is key to the meaning
of this passage? Why? _____

_____

_____

Which verse, sentence, or phrase bothers you or makes you stop and
think the most? What about it causes you to stop and think? _____

_____

_____

How can you apply Jesus' words in your life? How *will* you apply
what He has taught you? _____

_____

_____

Jesus' Stories
Mark 12:1-12

What title would you give this parable? _____

_____

_____

Why do you think Jesus tells this story? _____

_____

_____

What key message do you think Jesus wants to teach? _____

_____

_____

How will you apply Jesus' lesson in your life? _____

_____

_____

_____

Letters

2 Timothy 2:14-26

Who wrote the letter and to whom? _____

_____

Why did the author write this to the church? _____

_____

What are the key points? _____

_____

_____

What is the theme? _____

Is there a key verse? _____

How do you intend to apply this in your own life? _____

_____

_____

Verse Study
2 Chronicles 16:9

Paraphrase the passage—put it in your own words. _____

_____

_____

_____

Cross-reference the passage—find any other passages that help you
understand words or concepts. _____

_____

Record any insights you have gained. _____

_____

_____

_____

_____

How will you apply what you have learned? _____

_____

_____

_____

Sing to the Lord
Psalm 42

The overall message of this psalm is..._____

_____

Which line or couplet from this psalm speaks most powerfully to
you? Why? _____

_____

_____

Does any section in this psalm disturb you? Why? _____

_____

_____

Write down any promises of blessing and any promises of curses.

_____

_____

According to the psalm, what must you do to receive either the blessings or the curses? _____

Do any portions of this psalm serve as prophecy, either *forthtelling*
truths or *foretelling* future events? _____

How will you change as a result of this psalm? _____

_____

Jesus' Words

John 8:12-30

What are Jesus' key ideas in this passage? _____

_____

_____

_____

Which verse, sentence, or phrase do you think is key to the meaning
of this passage? Why? _____

_____

_____

Which verse, sentence, or phrase bothers you or makes you stop and
think the most? What about it causes you to stop and think? _____

_____

_____

How can you apply Jesus' words in your life? How *will* you apply
what He has taught you? _____

_____

_____

Jesus' Actions

Read the following passages and then fill in the blanks.

Passage	What did Jesus do?	Over what does He have power and authority?
Matthew 21:18-22		
Mark 2:3-14		
Matthew 17:24-27		
Mark 8:22-26		
John 11:1-44		
Mark 7:31-37		

Pray for Jesus to act in one of the areas in your own or someone else's life.

Day 5

Letters

Titus 3:1-11

Who wrote the letter and to whom? _____

_____

Why did the author write this to the church? _____

_____

What are the key points? _____

_____

_____

What is the theme? _____

Is there a key verse? _____

How do you intend to apply this in your own life? _____

_____

_____

Prayer
1 Chronicles 17:16-27

Who prays? _____

Why is the person praying? _____
_____

What happens as a result? _____
_____
_____

Write a prayer based on the pattern in the passage. _____
_____
_____
_____
_____
_____

Day 2

Wise Sayings
Proverbs 23:20,21

What analogies do these proverbs use? _____

_____

What attitude or action do these texts praise? _____

_____

What benefits does this proverb promise us if we follow its advice?

_____

What attitudes or actions do these texts condemn? _____

_____

What curses are we promised if we fail to heed their commands? ____

_____

The message of these proverbs is ... _____

_____

_____

_____

Jesus' Words

John 8:31-59

What are Jesus' key ideas in this passage? _____

_____

_____

_____

Which verse, sentence, or phrase do you think is key to the meaning
of this passage? Why? _____

_____

_____

Which verse, sentence, or phrase bothers you or makes you stop and
think the most? What about it causes you to stop and think? _____

_____

_____

How can you apply Jesus' words in your life? How *will* you apply
what He has taught you? _____

_____

_____

Jesus' Stories
Luke 12:13-34

What title would you give this parable? _____

_____

_____

Why do you think Jesus tells this story? _____

_____

_____

What key message do you think Jesus wants to teach? _____

_____

_____

How will you apply Jesus' lesson in your life? _____

_____

_____

_____

Sermons

Acts 17:16-34

Who was the preacher? _____

List the key points of the sermon. _____

_____

_____

_____

_____

Who was the audience? _____

How did the speaker tailor the sermon to the audience? _____

_____

_____

What was the response to the sermon? _____

_____

_____

Biography

Numbers 22-24

Describe the primary character. List his chief characteristics. _____

_____

_____

What events confirm your description? _____

_____

When does this person live? _____

Where does he live? _____

_____

Why do you think God included this person's biography in the Bible?

_____

_____

How do you intend to change as a result of studying this person? ____

_____

_____

Sing to the Lord
Psalm 43

The overall message of this psalm is..._____

_____

Which line or couplet from this psalm speaks most powerfully to you? Why? _____

_____

_____

Does any section in this psalm disturb you? Why? _____

_____

_____

Write down any promises of blessing and any promises of curses.

_____

_____

According to the psalm, what must you do to receive either the blessings or the curses? _____

Do any portions of this psalm serve as prophecy, either *forthtelling* truths or *foretelling* future events? _____

How will you change as a result of this psalm? _____

_____

Jesus' Words

John 10:1-21

What are Jesus' key ideas in this passage? _____

_____

_____

_____

Which verse, sentence, or phrase do you think is key to the meaning of this passage? Why? _____

_____

_____

Which verse, sentence, or phrase bothers you or makes you stop and think the most? What about it causes you to stop and think? _____

_____

_____

How can you apply Jesus' words in your life? How *will* you apply what He has taught you? _____

_____

_____

Verse Study

Luke 9:23-25

Paraphrase the passage—put it in your own words. _____

_____

_____

_____

Cross-reference the passage—find any other passages that help you understand words or concepts. _____

_____

Record any insights you have gained. _____

_____

_____

_____

_____

How will you apply what you have learned? _____

_____

_____

_____

Letters

Philemon

Who wrote the letter and to whom? _____

_____

Why did the author write this to the church? _____

_____

What are the key points? _____

_____

_____

What is the theme? _____

Is there a key verse? _____

How do you intend to apply this in your own life? _____

_____

_____

Verse Study

Genesis 50:20

Paraphrase the passage—put it in your own words. _____

_____

_____

_____

Cross-reference the passage—find any other passages that help you
understand words or concepts. _____

_____

Record any insights you have gained. _____

_____

_____

_____

_____

How will you apply what you have learned? _____

_____

_____

_____

Wise Sayings

Proverbs 16:32

What analogies does this proverb use? _____

_____

What attitude or action does this text praise? _____

_____

What benefits does this proverb promise us if we follow its advice?

_____

What attitudes or actions does this text condemn? _____

_____

What curses are we promised if we fail to heed its commands? _____

_____

The message of this proverb is . . . _____

_____

_____

_____

Jesus' Words
John 10:22-42

What are Jesus' key ideas in this passage? _____

_____

_____

_____

Which verse, sentence, or phrase do you think is key to the meaning
of this passage? Why? _____

_____

_____

Which verse, sentence, or phrase bothers you or makes you stop and
think the most? What about it causes you to stop and think? _____

_____

_____

How can you apply Jesus' words in your life? How *will* you apply
what He has taught you? _____

_____

_____

Jesus' Stories

Matthew 21:28-32

What title would you give this parable? _____

_____

_____

Why do you think Jesus tells this story? _____

_____

_____

What key message do you think Jesus wants to teach? _____

_____

_____

How will you apply Jesus' lesson in your life? _____

_____

_____

_____

Letters

Hebrews 7

Who wrote the letter and to whom? _____

_____

Why did the author write this to the church? _____

_____

What are the key points? _____

_____

_____

What is the theme? _____

Is there a key verse? _____

How do you intend to apply this in your own life? _____

_____

_____

Report the Story
Job 1, 2; 42:10-17

Who is this story about? (Who are the main characters?) _____

_____

What happens in the story? (What is the primary conflict?) _____

_____

_____

When does this event take place? _____

Where does it take place?_____

Why do you think God included it in the Bible? _____

_____

_____

How do you intend to change as a result of reading this story? _____

_____

_____

Sing to the Lord
Psalm 46

The overall message of this psalm is..._____

_____

Which line or couplet from this psalm speaks most powerfully to you? Why? _____

_____

_____

Does any section in this psalm disturb you? Why? _____

_____

_____

Write down any promises of blessing and any promises of curses.

_____

_____

According to the psalm, what must you do to receive either the blessings or the curses? _____

Do any portions of this psalm serve as prophecy, either *forthtelling* truths or *foretelling* future events? _____

How will you change as a result of this psalm? _____

_____

Jesus' Words

John 13:1-20

What are Jesus' key ideas in this passage? _____

_____

_____

_____

Which verse, sentence, or phrase do you think is key to the meaning
of this passage? Why? _____

_____

_____

Which verse, sentence, or phrase bothers you or makes you stop and
think the most? What about it causes you to stop and think? _____

_____

_____

How can you apply Jesus' words in your life? How *will* you apply
what He has taught you? _____

_____

_____

Biography

Luke 10:38-40; John 11:1-12:11

Describe the primary character. List her chief characteristics. _____

_____

_____

What events confirm your description? _____

_____

When does this person live? _____

Where does she live? _____

_____

Why do you think God included this person's biography in the Bible?

_____

_____

How do you intend to change as a result of studying this person? ____

_____

_____

Letters

Hebrews 11

Who wrote the letter and to whom? _____

_____

Why did the author write this to the church? _____

_____

What are the key points? _____

_____

_____

What is the theme? _____

Is there a key verse? _____

How do you intend to apply this in your own life? _____

_____

_____

Biography

1 Kings 17-2 Kings 2

Describe the primary character. List his chief characteristics. _____

_____

_____

What events confirm your description? _____

_____

When does this person live? _____

Where does he live? _____

_____

Why do you think God included this person's biography in the Bible?

_____

_____

How do you intend to change as a result of studying this person? _____

_____

_____

Wise Sayings
Proverbs 21:13 & 19:17

What analogies do these proverbs use? _____

_____

What attitude or action do these texts praise? _____

_____

What benefits do these proverbs promise us if we follow their advice?

_____

What attitudes or actions do these texts condemn? _____

_____

What curses are we promised if we fail to heed their commands? ____

_____

The message of these proverbs is . . . _____

_____

_____

_____

Jesus' Words
John 14:1-14

What are Jesus' key ideas in this passage? _____

_____

_____

_____

Which verse, sentence, or phrase do you think is key to the meaning
of this passage? Why? _____

_____

_____

Which verse, sentence, or phrase bothers you or makes you stop and
think the most? What about it causes you to stop and think? _____

_____

_____

How can you apply Jesus' words in your life? How *will* you apply
what He has taught you? _____

_____

_____

Jesus' Words
Matthew 25:31-46

What are Jesus' key ideas in this passage? _____

_____

_____

_____

Which verse, sentence, or phrase do you think is key to the meaning of this passage? Why? _____

_____

_____

Which verse, sentence, or phrase bothers you or makes you stop and think the most? What about it causes you to stop and think? _____

_____

_____

How can you apply Jesus' words in your life? How *will* you apply what He has taught you? _____

_____

_____

Letters

Hebrews 12:1-17

Who wrote the letter and to whom? _____

_____

Why did the author write this to the church? _____

_____

What are the key points? _____

_____

_____

What is the theme? _____

Is there a key verse? _____

How do you intend to apply this in your own life? _____

_____

_____

Laws

Exodus 23:1-9

Rewrite each law in your own words. _____

_____

_____

_____

_____

_____

_____

_____

What promise does God give for obedience? _____

_____

What punishment does God promise for disobedience? _____

_____

What rationale does God give for each commandment? _____

_____

_____

_____

_____

What law do you need to take more seriously? _____

_____

Sing to the Lord

Psalm 91

The overall message of this psalm is..._____

_____

Which line or couplet from this psalm speaks most powerfully to
you? Why? _____

_____

_____

Does any section in this psalm disturb you? Why? _____

_____

_____

Write down any promises of blessing and any promises of curses.

_____

_____

According to the psalm, what must you do to receive either the blessings or the curses? _____

Do any portions of this psalm serve as prophecy, either *forthtelling*
truths or *foretelling* future events? _____

How will you change as a result of this psalm? _____

_____

Jesus' Words

John 14:15-31

What are Jesus' key ideas in this passage? _____

_____

_____

_____

Which verse, sentence, or phrase do you think is key to the meaning
of this passage? Why? _____

_____

_____

Which verse, sentence, or phrase bothers you or makes you stop and
think the most? What about it causes you to stop and think? _____

_____

_____

How can you apply Jesus' words in your life? How *will* you apply
what He has taught you? _____

_____

_____

Read the Entire Story
Matthew 26:20-28:20

Write down one new insight. _____

_____

Write a prayer of thanksgiving for Jesus' work on your behalf. _____

_____

_____

_____

_____

_____

Letters

James 1

Who wrote the letter and to whom? _____

_____

Why did the author write this to the church? _____

_____

What are the key points? _____

_____

_____

What is the theme? _____

Is there a key verse? _____

How do you intend to apply this in your own life? _____

_____

_____

Verse Study

Joshua 24:14-15

Paraphrase the passage—put it in your own words. _____

_____

_____

_____

Cross-reference the passage—find any other passages that help you
understand words or concepts. _____

_____

Record any insights you have gained. _____

_____

_____

_____

_____

How will you apply what you have learned? _____

_____

_____

_____

Wise Sayings

Proverbs 2:2-6

What analogies does this proverb use? _____

_____

What attitude or action does this text praise? _____

_____

What benefits does this proverb promise us if we follow its advice?

_____

What attitudes or actions does this text condemn? _____

_____

What curses are we promised if we fail to heed its commands? _____

_____

The message of this proverb is . . . _____

_____

_____

_____

Jesus' Words

John 15

What are Jesus' key ideas in this passage? _____

_____

_____

_____

Which verse, sentence, or phrase do you think is key to the meaning
of this passage? Why? _____

_____

_____

Which verse, sentence, or phrase bothers you or makes you stop and
think the most? What about it causes you to stop and think? _____

_____

_____

How can you apply Jesus' words in your life? How *will* you apply
what He has taught you? _____

_____

_____

Jesus' Stories
Matthew 20:1-16

What title would you give this parable? _____

_____

_____

Why do you think Jesus tells this story? _____

_____

_____

What key message do you think Jesus wants to teach? _____

_____

_____

How will you apply Jesus' lesson in your life? _____

_____

_____

_____

Letters

1 Peter 3:8-22

Who wrote the letter and to whom? _____

_____

Why did the author write this to the church? _____

_____

What are the key points? _____

_____

_____

What is the theme? _____

Is there a key verse? _____

How do you intend to apply this in your own life? _____

_____

_____

Biography

Judges 6-7

Describe the primary character. List his chief characteristics. _____

_____

_____

What events confirm your description? _____

_____

When does this person live? _____

Where does he live? _____

_____

Why do you think God included this person's biography in the Bible?

_____

_____

How do you intend to change as a result of studying this person? ____

_____

_____

Sing to the Lord
Psalm 121

The overall message of this psalm is... _____

_____

Which line or couplet from this psalm speaks most powerfully to you? Why? _____

_____

_____

Does any section in this psalm disturb you? Why? _____

_____

_____

Write down any promises of blessing and any promises of curses.

_____

_____

According to the psalm, what must you do to receive either the blessings or the curses? _____

Do any portions of this psalm serve as prophecy, either *forthtelling* truths or *foretelling* future events? _____

How will you change as a result of this psalm? _____

_____

Jesus' Words

Luke 10:1-24

What are Jesus' key ideas in this passage? _____

_____

_____

_____

Which verse, sentence, or phrase do you think is key to the meaning
of this passage? Why? _____

_____

_____

Which verse, sentence, or phrase bothers you or makes you stop and
think the most? What about it causes you to stop and think? _____

_____

_____

How can you apply Jesus' words in your life? How *will* you apply
what He has taught you? _____

_____

_____

Verse Study
Matthew 11:28-30

Paraphrase the passage—put it in your own words. _____

_____

_____

_____

Cross-reference the passage—find any other passages that help you
understand words or concepts. _____

_____

Record any insights you have gained. _____

_____

_____

_____

_____

How will you apply what you have learned? _____

_____

_____

_____

Letters

1 John 4

Who wrote the letter and to whom? _____

_____

Why did the author write this to the church? _____

_____

What are the key points? _____

_____

_____

What is the theme? _____

Is there a key verse? _____

How do you intend to apply this in your own life? _____

_____

_____

Verse Study
Psalm 119:9,11

Paraphrase the passage—put it in your own words. _____

_____

_____

_____

Cross-reference the passage—find any other passages that help you
understand words or concepts. _____

_____

Record any insights you have gained. _____

_____

_____

_____

_____

How will you apply what you have learned? _____

_____

_____

_____

Prophecy

Please look at the Old Testament prophecies in context. Notice how the New Testament author refers to them. Is the Old Testament passage an obvious prophecy? Why or why not?

New Testament Passage	Old Testament Passage	What does the Old Testament passage predict concerning Jesus?	Obvious Prophecy? (Y/N)
Matthew 11:11-14	Malachi 4:5-6		
Matthew 12:14-21	Isaiah 42:1-4		
Matthew 13:10-15	Jeremiah 5:21; Isaiah 6:9-10		
Matthew 13:34-35	Psalm 78:2		
Matthew 21:1-7	Zechariah 9:9		
Matthew 26:31	Zechariah 13:7		
Matthew 26:14-16; 27:3-10	Zechariah 11:12, 13; Jeremiah 19:1-13; 32:6-9		
Matthew 27:33-34	Psalm 69:21		
Matthew 27:35	Psalm 22:18		
Matthew 27:46	Psalm 22:1		

Jesus' Words

Matthew 19:16-30

What are Jesus' key ideas in this passage? _____

_____

_____

_____

Which verse, sentence, or phrase do you think is key to the meaning
of this passage? Why? _____

_____

_____

Which verse, sentence, or phrase bothers you or makes you stop and
think the most? What about it causes you to stop and think? _____

_____

_____

How can you apply Jesus' words in your life? How *will* you apply
what He has taught you? _____

_____

_____

Jesus' Stories
Luke 18:1-8

What title would you give this parable? _____

_____

_____

Why do you think Jesus tells this story? _____

_____

_____

What key message do you think Jesus wants to teach? _____

_____

_____

How will you apply Jesus' lesson in your life? _____

_____

_____

_____

Letters

Revelation 5

Who wrote the letter and to whom? _____

_____

Why did the author write this to the church? _____

_____

What are the key points? _____

_____

_____

What is the theme? _____

Is there a key verse? _____

How do you intend to apply this in your own life? _____

_____

_____

Report the Story
1 Samuel 15:10-23

Who is this story about? (Who are the main characters?) _____

_____

What happens in the story? (What is the primary conflict?) _____

_____

_____

When does this event take place? _____

Where does it take place?_____

Why do you think God included it in the Bible? _____

_____

_____

How do you intend to change as a result of reading this story? _____

_____

_____

Sing to the Lord
Psalm 127

The overall message of this psalm is..._____

_____

Which line or couplet from this psalm speaks most powerfully to you? Why? _____

_____

_____

Does any section in this psalm disturb you? Why? _____

_____

_____

Write down any promises of blessing and any promises of curses.

_____

_____

According to the psalm, what must you do to receive either the blessings or the curses? _____

Do any portions of this psalm serve as prophecy, either *forthtelling* truths or *foretelling* future events? _____

How will you change as a result of this psalm? _____

_____

Jesus' Words
Acts 1:1-11

What are Jesus' key ideas in this passage? _____

_____

_____

_____

Which verse, sentence, or phrase do you think is key to the meaning
of this passage? Why? _____

_____

_____

Which verse, sentence, or phrase bothers you or makes you stop and
think the most? What about it causes you to stop and think? _____

_____

_____

How can you apply Jesus' words in your life? How *will* you apply
what He has taught you? _____

_____

_____

Verse Study

Matthew 28:19-20

Paraphrase the passage—put it in your own words. _____

_____

_____

_____

Cross-reference the passage—find any other passages that help you

understand words or concepts. _____

_____

Record any insights you have gained. _____

_____

_____

_____

_____

How will you apply what you have learned? _____

_____

_____

_____

Letters

Revelation 21:1-8

Who wrote the letter and to whom? _____

_____

Why did the author write this to the church? _____

_____

What are the key points? _____

_____

_____

What is the theme? _____

Is there a key verse? _____

How do you intend to apply this in your own life? _____

_____

_____